PAST AND PRESENT

REFUGEES

CAROLE SEYMOUR-JONES

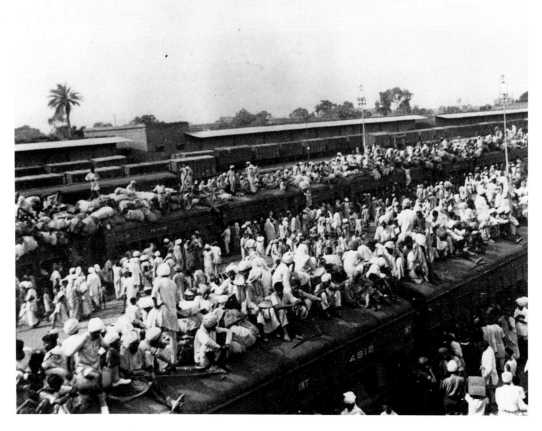

In 1947, India's borders changed when Pakistan was created as an independent Muslim state. Over nine million people found that they were on the wrong side of the border, and were forced to leave their homes. Refugees travelled in both directions — Muslims moved to the area which became Pakistan and non-Muslims left this area to live in India.

HEINEMANN

© Heinemann Educational Books Ltd, 1992

First published by Heinemann Children's Reference, 1992, a division of Heinemann Educational Books Ltd., Halley Court, Jordan Hill, Oxford OX2 8EJ.

OXFORD LONDON EDINBURGH
MADRID PARIS ATHENS BOLOGNA
MELBOURNE SYDNEY AUCKLAND SINGAPORE
TOKYO IBADAN NAIROBI GABORONE HARARE
PORTSMOUTH NH (USA)

Devised and produced by Zoë Books Limited
15 Worthy Lane, Winchester, SO23 7AB, England

Edited by Charlotte Rolfe
Picture research by Faith Perkins
Designed by Julian Holland

Printed in Hong Kong

A CIP catalogue record for this book is available from the British Library.

ISBN 0 431 00666 0

Photographic acknowledgements

The authors and publishers wish to acknowledge with thanks, the following photographic sources:
Mary Evans Picture Library pp 6; 7: FORMAT Partners Photo-Library pp16 (Brenda Prince); 35 (Jenny Matthews): Magnum pp 4 (Henri Cartier-Bresson); 15 (S.Salgado Jr.); 20 (Gideon Mendel); 28 (Chris Steele-Perkins); 37 (Raghu Rai): Peter Newark's American Pictures pp 9; 30: Popperfoto pp 19; 24; 26; 41; 44: Topham Picture Source pp title page, 22

Cover photograph courtesy of Magnum/M. Erwitt

The publishers have made every effort to trace the copyright holders, but if they have inadvertently overlooked any, they will be pleased to make the necessary arrangement at the first opportunity.

'TRAIL OF TEARS'

Sometimes people are pushed out of their own homes by another more powerful group. The struggle for land has been the cause of conflicts today and in the past. In the Americas many native peoples became refugees in their own country, as Europeans moved in with different ideas about land use and ownership.

The North American Cherokee Indians lived in and around the southern Appalachian mountains. They lived in small villages and practised agriculture. They adopted new farming techniques, and developed cotton and wool industries from the early European settlers in the area, and they had their own government. During the 1830s however, they lost huge amounts of land to the settlers in various treaties – the worst of which was the Treaty of New Echota (1835). Under this agreement, they were required to leave the land within three years. Although most Cherokee rejected the treaty, they were herded into camps and their homes were burnt. During the winter of 1838-39 they were marched by force to Indian Territory (now part of the state of Oklahoma), over 600 miles away. More than 15 000 Cherokee men, women and children made the journey, with little or nothing in the way of protection against hunger and the cold weather. About 4000 of them died on the way. Even the American soldiers guarding them described the conditions as terrible, and the journey became known as the 'Trail of Tears'.

KEEPING PEOPLE IN

People may also be stopped from travelling outside their country. A government may use its power to keep people within the country by not allowing them the necessary papers to travel – a passport for example. Those found trying to cross the border illegally may be imprisoned, or even executed. This kind of restriction on travel has been used in many countries, especially those where the government abuses human rights in order to keep itself in power.

When war breaks out between rival powers within a single country, the usual 'escape' routes such as ports and

The Berlin Wall was built in 1961 to stop skilled workers from the East crossing to prosperous West Germany. Originally it was a barbed-wire barricade, but by 1980, the Wall was 10ft (3.5m) high and more than 850 miles (1368km) long.

airports are quickly closed. People may be forced to find other ways of reaching safety. During the Spanish Civil War (1936-39) over half a million refugees fled across the mountains of the Pyrenees into France.

People living in one country may also want the freedom and improved living conditions they believe they can have somewhere else. This is what happened during the 1950s in communist East Germany. The escape route here was through Berlin. At the end of the Second World War, Berlin was occupied by the western powers (Britain, France and the United States) and the communist Soviet Union.

During the twenty or so years following the war, over two million East Germans crossed into West Berlin. This part of the city was under the protection of the western powers, and from here they could travel freely to resettle in West Germany or elsewhere.

Most of these people were highly skilled workers, which East Germany could ill afford to lose. By 1961 the East German government decided that direct action was needed to stop the flow. On the night of 13th August, police and soldiers sealed all the borders between East and West Berlin, and quickly put up a large barricade of barbed wire. Over the following days, a wall was built. It sealed East Berlin off from the West for the next 28 years.

During this time, a number of escape attempts were made. Some were successful, but 200 refugees lost their lives as they tried to cross the wall. They were shot dead by East German border guards under government orders. In 1989 the communist government in East Germany collapsed, and the wall was finally pulled down.

DRIVING PEOPLE OUT

In many countries, there are **ethnic minority** groups, who have settled for historical reasons. When Uganda became independent in 1962, there was a large Asian community living there. They had originally come from India to East Africa to help build the railways during colonial times, when the area was under British rule. Over the years they settled down with their families, many had started businesses, and had become quite prosperous. Like many minorities, however, they found that their position was not always certain, and their rights not fully protected in the newly-independent state.

> 'Uganda was my home. I had never been anywhere else. I was ten when I left on the aeroplane with my mother. My father promised he would follow us in a few days. I did not know if I would ever see him again.'
>
> *Asian refugee from Uganda,*
> *remembering 1972*

Early in 1971, the commander of the Ugandan army, Major-General Idi Amin, seized control of the country and ruled as a dictator for the next ten years. In 1972, he announced that all Asians would have to leave Uganda, and that their property should be taken over by African Ugandans. Over 30 000 Asian refugees took flights out of the country. Many of those who remained behind were murdered by Amin's soldiers.

Most of the refugees had British passports which had been issued to them at Uganda's independence. For this group there was a guaranteed entry into Britain. For the 6500 stateless Asians, the solution was not so straightforward, and some had the terrifying experience of being flown from one strange country to another in search of refuge. The international community made a great effort to resettle them, and many found new homes in the United States, Canada and elsewhere. However, the process took many painful months.

FLIGHT FROM STARVATION

In many countries in the world, people's lives depend closely on the animals they keep and the few crops they manage to grow. If they find themselves in the middle of a long war, as has happened to many ordinary people in Ethiopia for example, their entire livelihood can be destroyed and they face starvation unless they move out and search for a new chance somewhere else. If the disturbance of war combines with natural disasters such as drought, people's suffering is increased.

Although Africa has many fertile regions, the continent which in 1960 exported more food than it imported, today needs one billion dollars a year in food aid, and most African countries are on the UN list for emergency help. There are many reasons for this worsening situation, which has cost the lives of so many refugees:

- Desertification. This is partly due to drought, and partly the result of people cutting down trees for firewood. The Sahara desert today gallops south at a rate of 10 kilometres a year.
- High population growth. This means that more people compete for fewer resources such as agricultural land, food and water. In less than 30 years Sudan, Kenya and Nigeria will more than double their populations.

This child may spend many years in one of these temporary camps, set up to house thousands of environmental refugees who were driven from their homeland in Ethiopia by years of famine.

- Poor road and rail connections. This makes distribution of food aid, and essential agricultural supplies difficult in rural areas. (The problem is made worse when a corrupt government takes the aid that is meant for the people, or when the supply routes are attacked by warring armies).

Refugees who leave their homes for reasons such as drought or famine are known as environmental refugees. Many of them suffer in the poorest of camps on the edge of a town or city, with no hope of ever returning, and little chance of international refugee assistance.

A WARM WELCOME?

When the Communists took control of Vietnam, thousands of people fled to Hong Kong, already a densely populated country. To deter any further refugees, the 'boat people' were put into 'closed camps'. Many Vietnamese have lived in these squalid conditions in Hong Kong for seven years.

Most refugees face one main problem: will they be welcome in the **host country** to which they flee? In poorer countries, it may not be easy to look after extra numbers of people making demands on jobs, living space, social services and other scarce resources. Existing inhabitants of the country may feel that the new arrivals are competing with them for these things.

In the rich countries of the world, people sometimes also talk about being 'swamped' by unwanted **immigrants,** especially those of a different cultural background. Newcomers may find that they are automatically blamed for many of the problems in the new country, such as housing shortages, crime and racial tension. Small numbers of refugees, with some means of supporting themselves may be welcomed into the community; but when large numbers of poor people seek refuge and a new start in life, host governments begin to react differently.

CLOSING THE DOOR IN SOUTH-EAST ASIA

In 1975, the city of Saigon finally fell to the communist forces in the last stages of the Vietnam War. Thousands of Vietnamese risked their lives to cross the sea to safety, often in small insecure fishing boats. They were joined by people from neighbouring countries such as Laos and Cambodia. These countries had also been thrown into disorder by the years of war in the region. By 1978, 86 000 'boat people' as they became known, had arrived in Thailand, and other south-east Asian countries.

The Thai government was dismayed. Its leader, Premier Kriangsak, said that Thailand was not being 'flooded' by refugees, it was being 'drowned', as thousands of fare-paying Vietnamese arrived in charter ships. The government began to **screen** or check arrivals, in order to find out who were 'real' refugees, 'with a well-founded fear of being persecuted' as the 1951 UN Convention on Refugees put it. They suspected that many people simply came in search of a better life, and they labelled these people **economic refugees.**

Different countries used a variety of ways to keep

States took in waves of European refugees who fled to a new life from revolution and two world wars. In more recent years, Israel went one step further in rescuing the Jewish inhabitants of Ethiopia, a country devastated by war and famine.

The Falashas as they are known (the word means 'stranger') had lived in this part of Africa for centuries. No-one knows how they first came to Ethiopia, although the Falashas believe they are descended from those who returned to Africa with the Queen of Sheba after she visited Jerusalem during the tenth century BC.

At the beginning of the twentieth century there were 100 000 Falashas in Ethiopia, but as a small, separate community they suffered at the hands of various Ethiopian governments; they were murdered, tortured, and sold into slavery. They now number only 20 000.

This Falasha grandmother, rescued from persecution in Ethiopia by 'Operation Solomon', has great difficulty in adjusting to the housing and facilities in Israel, after a completely different way of life in Africa.

In 1971 the American Association for Ethiopian Jewry began the campaign for a rescue operation to remove the Falashas to safety in Israel. The first secret airlift took place in 1985. In 1991, 'Operation Solomon' was mounted: 14 000 Ethiopian Jews were flown to Israel from Ethiopia's capital city, Addis Ababa. It was the biggest air rescue operation in Israeli history.

On reaching Israel, the Ethiopian refugees faced a culture shock. Within hours, they found themselves removed from a simple life of farming which had not changed much for thousands of years, and had to face the newness of modern Israeli living – with a strange diet, packaged food, western style housing, and a language and lifestyle completely unknown to them.

Nevertheless, the new Ethiopian-Israelis are fortunate because they possess the documents necessary in the twentieth century world: identity cards or passports giving proof of nationality. Without these, a person is stateless, unacceptable to the countries he or she may wish to enter. If a stateless person arrives by air or sea he or she will be turned back. Without identity papers there is no way out of a refugee camp, no means of building a new life.

> 'There is little historical evidence to support the argument that most refugees are deterred by the threat of inhumane treatment on arrival – which they have too often received – when the need to leave their own country has been compelling.'
>
> *Dennis MacNamara, UNHCR, 1990*

HOW TO HELP?

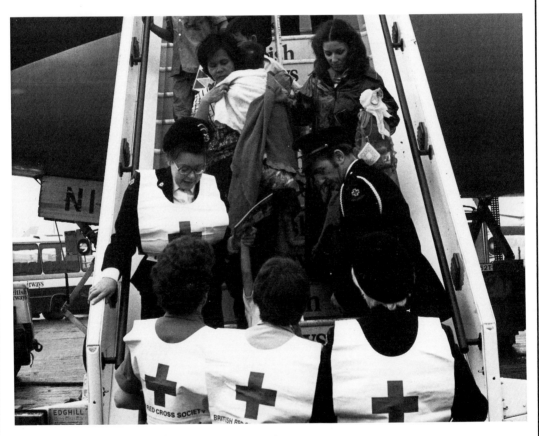

The Swiss businessman, Henri Dunant, was so moved by the
horror of seeing thousands of wounded soldiers left to die on
an Italian battlefield that he set up the first 'Voluntary Aid
Society' in 1863. This became the Red Cross. Over a century
later, British members of this now worldwide organization,
welcome Vietnamese refugees as they arrive in London.

Since the Second World War, international organizations have been developed to protect refugees. The United Nations High Commission for Refugees (UNHCR) co-operates with national governments and voluntary organizations such as the Red Cross or Red Crescent, Oxfam, Christian Aid, and Save the Children Fund. These voluntary organizations claim to be non-political and unbiased, non-profit making, and to have experience with the 'grassroots' which makes them the best agencies to help displaced people. Certainly most of these organizations are sincere and well-intentioned in their efforts, but it is doubtful whether they alone can solve what has become a world problem.

'Many people still attempt to approach the refugee problem... as if it were a charity. This attitude will never be enough to meet the problems of the 1990s.'

UN High Commissioner for Refugees, 1990

WORK OR REFUGE?

In the 1950s, Europe, struggling to recover from two wars, quickly absorbed refugees and displaced people from central and eastern Europe. In the 1960s western governments had a shortage of labour, and as a result 10 million **guest-workers** were recruited from southern Europe. Refugees from the dictatorships of Greece, Spain and Portugal, were easily absorbed in countries which required their labour and skills.

But as the refugee crisis in south-east Asia showed, by the 1980s, the situation had changed. In 1985 19 million people were unemployed in western Europe, and individual countries began to question whether they had room for large numbers of Asian immigrants. In the 1980s the total European intake of refugees for one year was 850 000, while the United States and Canada took another 700 000. In 1985 there was a turning-point. For the first time the number of refugees seeking asylum was greater than the number of legally admitted foreign workers.

WHOSE AID? WHOSE INTERESTS?

Some people argue that the various organizations set up to solve the refugee problems of today are not in a position to do always what is best for the refugees. These organizations depend on the rich countries of Europe and North America, and on Japan and Australia, for their financial and political support. National interests, as we have seen, may simply be to keep people out. In many of these countries there are **racist** pressure groups or political parties who argue that people should be stopped from entering the country simply on the ground of their race, or colour.

A second criticism of the refugee organizations is that they do not respond to refugee problems until too late. In the case of the Kurds who fled the Iraqis during the 1991 Gulf War, international help was slow to come. Only when the world's media has drawn attention to suffering does

Not all immigrants are welcome in their adopted countries. This young Turkish immigrant in Belgium is pointing at an election poster for an extremist party. The slogan reads 'For self-defence. Our own people first'.

the West offer financial aid. The refugee organizations themselves argue that they have learnt much in the last 30 years. Instead of handouts of food and medical relief and welfare payments to refugees, they have moved into setting up development projects which have the aim of helping people who might otherwise become environmental refugees.

THE CAMP SYSTEM: HAS ANYTHING CHANGED?

The 'we know what's best for them' approach to refugees is still seen in refugee camps, which are often created for the sake of convenience. In camps it is easier to count refugees, to deliver aid, and to control food distribution. Also people and governments are more likely to give money to refugees when they are visible in camps, and can be photographed, than when they are settled in a host society. But what do the refugees themselves think?

'Refugees generally dislike camps and avoid them as much as possible. They tend to use them only as a "safety net" when all else fails, as support for their most vulnerable family members, or where there are security problems.'

Refugee Participation Network, 1991

A list of camp dangers might read:
1 Health risk: camp populations are exposed to disease
2 Unemployment: there is often no work for camp populations
3 Dependency: camp populations lose control over their own lives
4 Local hostility: local communities dislike camps in their midst, which strain local resources
5 Integration into host country is more difficult in camps.

These dangers are well known. The 1982 UNHCR Handbook advises field officers only to establish camps as a last resort. Nevertheless, because refugees are so often

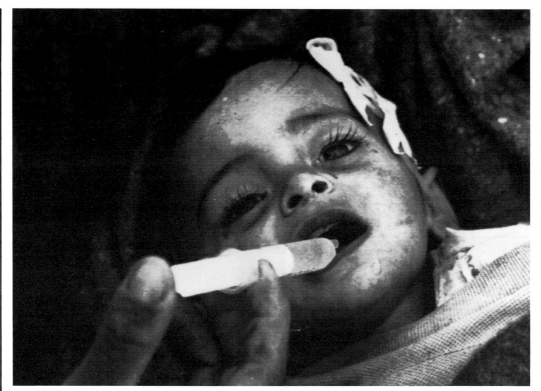

This Kurdish baby is being fed glucose to help stop the effects of dehydration. The lack of water in the Turkish refugee camps, set up after the Gulf War, has meant that many people living there suffer from dehydration.

powerless victims of circumstances, they often find themselves in camps against their will. In a survival situation they have no choice.

Since the state of Israel was founded in 1948 many Palestinian Arabs previously living in the area have ended up in refugee camps run by the United Nations Relief and Works Agency (UNRWA). In the 1948-49 war between the new state of Israel and its Arab neighbours, 750 000 small landowners, farm workers and labourers lost their homes and jobs. They fled from the territory which became the state of Israel to surrounding areas such as the West Bank, the Gaza Strip, and neighbouring Arab countries such as Jordan, Lebanon and Syria.

In the 1967 Arab-Israeli war, another 500 000

Palestinians lost their homes in the territories occupied by Israel. In 1988, the fortieth anniversary of the Universal Declaration of Human Rights, the Palestinians began the *intifadah* or uprising against Israeli occupation of the West Bank and Gaza Strip. The United Nations condemned Israel for 'violating the human rights of Palestinian people in the occupied Palestinian territories, including Jerusalem.' The Commission on Human Rights in 1988 also condemned Israel's use of violence. But although the UN recognizes the rights of the Palestinian people to govern themselves and to have national independence, its pronouncements seem to have little effect. The Palestinian **diaspora** has lasted 40 years.

One example of life in a Palestinian camp shows what everyday life can be like. Saffiyeh Hamdan and her seven children live in Nuseirat Camp, Gaza, in a two-room shelter. Her son, aged 20, is the breadwinner, bringing home about 20 shekels a day (about 10 US dollars) for picking oranges for eight hours. However if there is a curfew, he cannot work. UNRWA gives these refugees flour and skimmed milk rations. The children fight and quarrel, as the UNRWA schools are shut while the curfew lasts. They cannot leave their home for fear of army patrols.

SKILLS TRAINING AND EDUCATION

In order to give refugees self-respect and to help them to support themselves, some organizations run training programmes in refugee camps, such as Beqa'a, 20 kilometres north of Amman. This is the largest Palestinian refugee camp in Jordan. Most families here do not like their wives and daughters to work outside the camp in factories, but allow them to make school uniforms, nurses' gowns and chefs' uniforms at the vocational training centre. Not only does this give them an income, it also helps them feel less dependent and isolated.

Refugees prize education as a way out of camps for their children. UNRWA runs 631 schools for the Palestinians, and provides university scholarships. In Beqa'a camp there is a nursery school for 380 children and a programme

Civil war in El Salvador has made thousands homeless. Refugee camps have become permanent home for these people. This camp near San Salvador houses 800 refugees. Although few facilities exist, education continues and these boys show that classroom habits are the same everywhere, no matter where lessons are held.

for women on health and child care and women's rights. As women and children form the majority of refugees in the world today, training and study programmes have been geared towards their needs.

NO WAY OUT

In 1978 thousands of nomads fled civil war in Ethiopia. Having lost most of their herds of cattle, they were organized into 35 camps in Somalia containing over a million refugees. Being settled in one place brought dramatic changes to the lifestyle and diet of the nomads: instead of meat and milk they had to eat inadequate cereal rations. Diseases such as scurvy and anaemia broke out, because of lack of vitamin C and iron. In one camp alone 60 women died of bleeding during childbirth due to severe anaemia.

There were problems in keeping the camps clean and healthy. Diseases such as malaria and measles spread, because of overcrowding. Because the numbers of refugees were not accurately counted, it was difficult to obtain enough food from donors, who thought the figures were exaggerated and sent less food. Families who did not have 'ghost members' or surplus ration cards went short of food, especially females.

LESSONS LEARNED?

The experience of dealing with ever greater numbers of refugees, and the knowledge of conditions in long-term refugee camps, has helped many of the refugee organizations to improve their efforts and to give more appropriate support. But it is still difficult to predict a massive movement of people, or to obtain enough help in advance to deal with the problem. A flow of refugees can occur very quickly, as often happens in a war or a natural disaster. Relief organizations know that it can take many months to organize essential supplies, and that people are more at risk at certain times of the year, such as during cold winter months, or during a hot dry season. Yet their warnings about future crises are not always heeded.

CROSSING OVER

These immigrants, arriving in America about 1900, were typical of the millions who sought a better life in the 'land of plenty'. Ellis Island, New York, was the nation's major immigration centre from 1892 to 1943.

Losing one's home and country, friends and familiar culture through flight can feel like losing a close relative or friend through death. Feelings of great sadness and regret may mingle with anger and despair. It takes time to adjust or 'cross over' to the new life, and for many, the experience leaves a permanent scar.

THINKING ABOUT THE PAST

Refugees are all individuals with their own personal past or 'ghost reality'. This 'ghost reality' is often the main barrier to settling down and becoming part of a new society. It can sometimes appear as an escape from the problems of coping with a new and different way of life.

One woman who fled to Australia from her island home in East Timor, Indonesia, explains how her memories of the past affected her abilities to get on with her new life:

'I survive the present by living in the past and only the future will tell me how well I have coped.... I was probably dreaming but it was a painful daylight dream – one about the past which is now a lost present; family, language, job, culture and country. It was a cloudy dream in which I had no sense of direction and time. Though I knew I had always been confident of my moves, this time I was losing control over my existence – I started to feel powerless and very dependent on my friends.'

For many refugees, the past contains horrific memories. Fourteen-year old May risked her life when she and her sisters left Vietnam in a refugee boat with 22 other passengers. The boat was attacked by pirates, and six women, including May and her sisters, were captured and sexually abused. May was separated from her sisters and transferred to another fishing boat. Then she was thrown into the sea, where she drifted for a day and a half before being rescued by a marine police boat and brought ashore. She has never seen her sisters again.

May told the police what had happened, and was able to remember the number of the fishing boat, which led to the pirates' arrest. However, at the identification parade she was too terrified to identify her attackers. After a seven month waiting period in a refugee camp May settled in the

United States, but she has never had any further news of her family. She has had to make a new life alone in the world, apart from the support of her counsellor and the authorities.

FACING THE FUTURE

Every refugee's goal is to make a new home either in the country to which he or she flees, or in another third country. Sometimes, sadly, the half-way house of camp life becomes permanent, as it has done for many Palestinians, and for over three million Afghans in Pakistan. Sometimes refugees return to their country of origin, as some Vietnamese have done. But getting out of the camps and tackling day-to-day problems is the first step along the road towards **integration** – becoming part of a new society.

FITTING IN

At various times in the sixteenth and seventeenth centuries, Protestant refugees from continental Europe sought safety in England. Although these exiles set up their own churches, like the French Protestant church in Threadneedle Street in the City of London, they soon became integrated into English society. This was partly because they brought welcome skills such as silk-weaving and glass-blowing.

Many Protestants also emigrated to North America. In 1621 Philippe de la Noye, a Huguenot, arrived at Plymouth, Massachusetts, on the *Fortune;* one of his

'The poor exiles from Flanders, France and other countries... are our brethren; they live not idly. If they have houses of us, they pay us rent for them... they beg not in our streets... they labour truthfully, they live sparingly. They are good examples of virtue, travail, faith and patience.'

John Jewell,
English bishop (1522-71)

descendants was Franklin D. Roosevelt. In 1629 another Huguenot, Baron de Sauce, sailed from France to Virginia where he established a settlement of Huguenots; many Virginian families today have French surnames, such as Battaille or Vicomte.

During the nineteenth century and the years leading up to the First World War (1914-18) over 32 million people emigrated to the United States. Many were fleeing from war, persecution or famine. After the Second World War, there was a further wave of refugees, mainly from central and eastern Europe. For most of this group, there was an important hurdle to cross: language. One young German refugee describes his experience in the early 1950s:

'My father had been killed in the war, and there was no future for us in Germany. After some time in a refugee camp, we sailed to America, where my mother got a job helping her old professor from Berlin – he had fled to America before the war. My two brothers and I stayed at a children's home, where we were separated and made to speak English from the start. I was nine years old, and I found it very hard.'

Speaking the language of the host country is perhaps the most important key to integrating into its society. It helps the newcomer to deal with other challenges such as finding work and a place to live. Other factors such as race, religion, and political views also affect the way in which an individual fits into a new country. Many refugees form their own communities as a natural way of preserving their own traditions, and giving each other support when necessary.

INTEGRATING IN AUSTRIA
In 1956 after the Hungarian revolution, which was crushed by the Communists, 200 000 refugees fled to Austria, and Traiskirchen became the country's main reception and **transit camp,** helping people prepare for their new lives. In 1982, 25 000 Poles also sought asylum in Traiskirchen, by then the biggest refugee camp in Europe.

Today, it provides a minimum of accommodation, food

and free medical care for 11 000 Romanians, as well as Bulgarians and others who crossed from eastern Europe to the West, before and after the fall of the Berlin Wall in 1989. In 1990 there were over 43 nationalities in the camp. They spoke English, German, Flemish, French, Italian, Romanian, Hungarian, Iranian, Yugoslavian, Bulgarian and Turkish.

As a result, communication is not easy. As one camp leader has noted, 'Sometimes the only possible language that can be used is the body language, but one always uses the heart language.' To prepare refugees for integration there are special language courses. For the many who settle in Austria, it is essential to learn German. Films are shown about the other countries to which refugees may emigrate, such as the United States, Canada, Australia, Britain, Israel, and Scandinavia.

Children may be quicker than their parents in adapting to a new culture. At Traiskirchen, they go to Austrian schools, and have their own camp programme of art and craft. Summercamps have been used for many years at Traiskirchen, as a way of removing the children, for a while at least, from the tension of camp life. As the camp director wrote in 1952, 'We tried... to make them forget for a while the disappointment and frustration of postponed emigration schemes, the overcrowding of barrack life, blackmarketeering, stealing etc., habits into which many of the refugees have fallen.' Reconciling national groups to each other is also an important task in the camp. Different nationalities may fear and hate each other, just as they feel fear of the unknown outside the camp.

Yet these European refugees are perhaps the lucky ones, for they represent only 5 percent of refugees worldwide in 1991, and there is an efficient system in operation to help them lay at rest the ghosts of the past. Racism is not a major problem in integrating Europeans from one country into another. In the poorer countries of the Third World the picture is bleaker, the problems different, the numbers far greater. Host countries themselves may be hard pressed to provide all the extra help needed.

These women are being taught to read and write in a camp in Eritrea, a province of Ethiopia. Eritrea wants independence from Ethiopia and rival factions fight bitterly among themselves about the best way to achieve this. Villagers seek refuge in camps but, even during lessons, weapons stay within reach.

INTEGRATING IN SWAZILAND

Since most refugees do not want to be dependent on aid, they stay out of camps if possible. In 1984, there were 14 500 refugees from the fighting in Mozambique, living in camps. The camps were isolated and jobs were scarce. Trading was difficult because the refugees were poor and the camps were far away from markets. By contrast, the large numbers of Mozambicans (estimates vary from 60 000 to 134 000) who settled in the border areas of neighbouring Swaziland worked out their own ways to survive. Local villagers lent them small plots of land to cultivate, and they also worked for local farmers as day labourers.

The refugees provided cheap labour for the small-scale farmers who were able to increase production. When drought came to Swaziland in 1987, the government began a border feeding programme of maize and beans for the refugees who were registered with host families. Each family was given a ration card.

However, after October 1990, the refugees were told that if they wanted to continue receiving food, they would have to move into Malindza refugee camp. The border feeding programme was to be phased out at the height of the hungry season. The refugees moved to the camp unwillingly – they knew they were losing freedom and dignity and becoming dependent on handouts. Some saw Malindza as 'a death trap, a place of no hope'.

Local Swazi chiefs resented the fact that the food programme was stopped without their agreement, and the refugees removed to the camp. They wanted the refugees to be registered so that they could keep track of their movements. 'Before, the refugees were with us, under our care, but now they are under UNHCR... How can we trust them?'

All these events in Swaziland showed how the refugees were better off when actively contributing to their own survival, and working within a community. Once they were removed to a camp, they lost the trust and co-operation of the local people, as well as their own freedom.

SHARING THE PROBLEM

Over 40 years ago, China sent in 40 000 troops to occupy Tibet. Many people, including the Dalai Lama, the spiritual leader of Tibet, fled to India and are still living there. In 1987, Tibetans in Dharamsala, Northern India, demonstrated in support of anti-Chinese riots in Lhasa, the capital of Tibet.

The refugee situation in the world today is reaching crisis point – the numbers of refugees have doubled in the last ten years alone. The organizations set up to help them over 40 years ago are no longer able to cope with the sheer size of the problem. Why is this happening?

THE NORTH-SOUTH GAP

In the big-spending 1970s, many poorer countries were encouraged by international banks to take out huge loans to finance their development. The idea was that they should 'catch up' with the rich countries of the world. But over the years they had to pay higher prices for key products such as oil and machinery, while the sums they received from their own produce stayed the same or even dropped. Today, many of the world's poorest countries are crippled by international debts, and are unable to feed their own growing populations. In 1991, these countries paid out more money in debt repayments, than they received in aid from the rich North.

The problem of debt is made worse by a rapidly increasing population. Most population growth is taking place in the developing countries, which is likely to result in more and more people being unable to feed themselves. One billion people in the world are hungry today – that is one person in five. This number will continue to rise as world population rockets from 5.1 billion today, to possibly 8.5 billion in the year 2050. As we have seen, poverty uproots people, who may flee their homes and come knocking on the doors of the rich countries of the North.

SUPERPOWERS AT WAR

Many of the wars that have taken place in the last 40 years have been encouraged by the world's most powerful nations. People have lost their homes and livelihood. Neighbouring countries have had to carry a refugee burden they can ill afford. Opposing sides in wars in Ethiopia, Somalia and the Sudan for example, were backed by either the former Soviet Union or the western powers in a struggle for power and influence in the area.

International aid may not reach the innocent victims caught in the crossfire of these conflicts. In a drawn out civil war in Ethiopia, General Mengistu and his government diverted food aid to his own soldiers. He also increased the refugee problem by forcing villagers out of their homes and by spending large amounts of government money on a war against a section of his own population.

Sometimes the link between superpower ambition and a long-term refugee problem is more direct, for example when a superpower itself invades a neighbouring country. Just over 40 years ago, communist China invaded Tibet and imposed its own government on the people there. Many Tibetans fled to India and Nepal and have not returned to their home country since. More recently, in 1979, the invasion of Afghanistan by the former Soviet Union sent many Afghans fleeing across the mountains into Pakistan. Many paid their life savings to guides who smuggled them across the border. Thanks to the

These Afghani children, huddled around a plate of food, are among the 14 000 Afghans living in this refugee camp in Pakistan.

generosity of their hosts and fellow Muslims, they are not the poorest of the world's refugees. Yet half of all Afghan refugees are children who have never seen Afghanistan. Although Soviet troops withdrew from their country in 1989, no mass return has taken place since. Afghans are fearful of going back to houses and lands ruined after the ten-year war.

The Gulf War of 1991 was an international conflict of a rather different kind. What started as an invasion of the oil state of Kuwait by its neighbour, Iraq, grew into a short but shattering desert war which involved the armed forces of a number of western countries, including the United States and Britain. People argue as to whether the West was defending the freedom of Kuwait as an independent state, or simply fighting to recapture its valuable oil supplies.

The Iraqi invasion meant that wealthy Kuwaitis had to flee their country or risk death. It also destroyed the livelihood of many foreign workers in Kuwait from poorer countries such as India and the Philippines. These people lost everything. They waited for many weeks at overflowing refugee centres often with little or no shelter, until arrangements could be made to transport them back to their countries of origin.

Long after the war itself was over and the Iraqi forces had been forced to withdraw behind their own borders, the lives of many civilians in the area were still shattered. The Kuwaitis began to return home to try and rebuild their country; but many ordinary Iraqis found that they were also refugees. Their homes had been destroyed by the war, or by armed attacks from a government choosing this time to show its strength at home by cracking down on the human rights of sections of its own population. Many wait without hope in refugee camps in neighbouring Iran. For them, the war has brought neither victory nor freedom.

The Gulf War shows how people, places and the world's resources are all interlinked – and that the resulting refugee situation is part of that pattern. It is not a problem that belongs to 'another' part of the world.

This Kurdish child is a victim of the Gulf War. He is one of thousands housed in camps along the Turkish border who relied on food rations dropped by US military helicopters.

ATTITUDES AT HOME

As television programmes have highlighted refugee stories across the world, it seems that attitudes in the democratic countries of the West are changing.

> 'Give me your tired, your poor, your huddled masses yearning to breath free...'
>
> *Statue of Liberty inscription,*
> *New York*

This was how refugees from Europe were once made welcome in the New World. But today, the old definitions of the word 'refugee' are crumbling. The 1951 Convention which defined a refugee as a person with a 'well-founded fear of persecution by reasons of race, religion, nationality, membership of a particular social group or political opinion' was intended to apply to Europeans after the Second World War, although in 1967 it was extended to refugees in other parts of the world. Its creators never envisaged the exploding statistics of refugees now in transit throughout the world.

Definitions become blurred, as people argue over whether refugees are 'political', 'economic', 'environmental' or perhaps all three. The term 'asylum-seeker' is used more commonly now, meaning one who seeks a safe refuge.

International law recognizes the right of a person to seek asylum but does not oblige countries to provide it. Many 'invisible refugees' exist too, people who have been displaced within their countries because of war or eviction, but who are not registered as refugees by their governments or UNHCR.

Desperation forces people to flee to the West illegally. Western countries still attract refugees because of higher living standards and the promise of freedom from persecution. The revolution in communications has made flight by air a popular choice for asylum-seekers.

Countries protect themselves against the world outside through control of their borders. In the United States over one million people were arrested in 1990 trying to cross the border with Mexico. Razor wire, dogs, helicopters and police keep out the 'illegal aliens', as the US Immigration

Service calls them, fleeing from El Salvador, Guatemala, Honduras, Mexico and Nicaragua. Most of the migrants were Mexicans, of who 15 were shot in 1990. Despite all the efforts of the border patrols, two out of three succeeded in their bid to reach the United States.

'FORTRESS EUROPE'

In 1991 the communist government finally collapsed in the Soviet Union, and the country disintegrated into a commonwealth of independent republics. Here and in eastern Europe, where communism was abandoned, old conflicts among different ethnic groups sometimes reappeared. In the case of Yugoslavia a bitter civil war broke out between the Serbians and Croatians.

In an atmosphere of uncertainty about the future, many people from eastern Europe flocked to the West. The number of asylum-seekers rose from 13 000 in 1972 to 420 000 in 1990, and nearly half of these came to Germany. Some groups have begun attacking foreigners, particularly guest-workers, who they think take jobs from Germans.

Twenty thousand Albanians have fled to Italy since 1990 and the Italian government says it can absorb no more. In Switzerland, low-paid hotel workers have included asylum-seekers from Yugoslavia, Turkey and the Middle East. As a result of the world recession in 1990 and 1991, jobs became scarce, and many immigrants were simply sent home.

Similarly in Britain doors are being closed. Tamils fleeing civil war in Sri Lanka made news when they were turned away by immigration officials in 1987. Ravi Sundralingam arrived with a forged passport and visa. His brother had already been shot in Sri Lanka and he had been tortured. When he was returned to Sri Lanka he was tortured again.

As the barriers fall within the European Community they are erected ever higher against refugees from outside. Countries claim 'ownership' of their citizens, to whom they grant passports as a privilege. Without a passport, no freedom of movement is possible, and the state can deny

When they saw the changes taking place elsewhere in eastern Europe, thousands tried to escape the oppression they still had to endure in their own country, Albania. In 1990, huge crowds of Albanian refugees scrambled onto boats to escape across the Adriatic Sea to Italy.

or confiscate passports at will. Today, airlines bringing passengers to Britain without valid visas face severe fines; thus the government is asking airline staff to operate as immigration officials. Asylum-seekers pay sums they often cannot afford to traders in forged documents – up to

£3000 a head for a European country.

Europe's control of its borders is extremely efficient. Only 0.17 percent of the population of western Europe is made up of refugees. As the North-South gap widens, the jealous countries of Europe are likely to become even more careful guardians of their wealth and privilege in **'Fortress Europe'.** New laws on immigration are under discussion in a number of European countries.

FINDING A WAY

As the poverty gap widens and the growing world population has unequal shares in the world's wealth, the refugee problem seems almost impossible to solve. But a start can be made if the rich countries of the North and the poor countries of the South act together to find solutions.

In the short term, the rich nations could support the relief organizations more generously. In the longer term, they could cancel the crippling debts and encourage development that is actually useful to the countries of the South, and doesn't reduce them to mere providers of raw materials. There is also the constant need to improve and maintain human rights, which are still ignored and abused in many parts of the world.

'Our willingness to tackle one of the greatest humanitarian challenges of this century is not only a test of our commitment to human rights and our belief in the fundamental worth of the human person; it is also a step towards building a better and safer world'.

UN High Commissioner for Refugees, 1991

Refugees throughout the world share a common humanity. Any one of us might be suddenly forced to flee our home for reasons beyond our control. Then, like the Kurdish man who held out the body of his dead baby son to the cameraman who came to film him in the mountains of Kurdistan, we might also cry in pain: 'Why? Why? Why has the world abandoned us?'

KEY DATES

1280 BC
Flight of a nation Moses leads the Israelites from Egypt to seek the Promised Land of Palestine (Canaan).

AD 1214
War displaces people Emperor Genghis Khan and Mongol army take Beijing and overrun China.

1685
First recorded use of the word 'refugee' Louis XIV forces French Protestants (Huguenots) to flee to England as *réfugiés*.

1780
First recorded use of word 'refugee' in the United States Applied to fleeing supporters of George III during American War of Independence.

1838-9
Expulsion of a people Trail of Tears on which 4000 Cherokees die when they are driven from their lands.

1921
Protection for stateless people Nansen passport devised by Dr Fridtjof Nansen, High Commissioner for Refugees, fails to protect refugees after the First World War.

1948
Whose homeland? The state of Israel is created but displaces in turn the Palestinians, of whom 2.5 million become refugees.

1951
Definition of refugees UN Convention on the Status of Refugees gives people the right to apply for asylum and show they are political refugees fleeing persecution. This definition, framed to protect European refugees after the Second World War, is expanded to apply to refugees world-wide in 1967.

1961
Keeping people in Berlin Wall built to prevent East Germans escaping to the West.

1972
Expulsion of an ethnic minority Idi Amin expels 27 000 Ugandan Asians.

1975
Escape by sea Following the fall of South Vietnamese capital Saigon to the Communists, Vietnamese, Cambodian and Laotian 'boat people' flee to Thailand and surrounding countries. They are labelled 'economic' refugees.

1978
Drought and famine create refugees People fleeing starvation because of drought in the Sahel are labelled 'environmental' refugees.

1991
Rescue story 'Operation Solomon' transports Ethiopian Jews (Falashas) to safety in Israel.

GLOSSARY

asylum Shelter and protection afforded by a *host country* to a refugee.

civil war War between opposing groups inside a country.

diaspora The scattering of a people throughout the world, usually as a result of war, persecution or economic reasons.

economic refugee Someone who is considered to be on the move not because of persecution but who simply seeks higher living standards afforded elsewhere.

emigrant Someone who leaves one country to live permanently in another, for any reason.

ethnic minority Group which differs in race (and possibly religion) from most of the population.

forced repatriation Returning someone as a prisoner, by force, to his or her country of origin.

'Fortress Europe' Expression describing the growing policy of European nations to tighten immigration policies and border controls to deter refugees from entering their countries.

guest-workers Immigrants, mainly from southern Europe encouraged by governments in the 1960s and 1970s to fill job vacancies in northern Europe.

host country The country which receives a refugee, either on a temporary or permanent basis.

human rights Basic rights of all human beings including freedom of personal beliefs and speech.

immigrant Someone who settles in a new country having left their country of birth or origin.

integration Fitting in with a local community, and the wider society of which it is a part.

'push and pull' factors Reasons which drive a person to flee, such as famine, persecution, and war, and attract them to a host country, such as religious freedom, jobs, better living standards.

racist Emphasising differences or encouraging hatred between races or ethnic groups.

refugee Someone forced to seek safety elsewhere, usually in a foreign country, in order to escape persecution, or as a result of a national disaster.

screening Questioning new arrivals in a country to find out more about them, for example, whether they are at risk in their home country.

stateless Having no nationality or citizenship; in particular having no papers such as a passport or identity card as proof of nationality.

transit camp Temporary camp in which a refugee awaits processing for resettlement in third country or return to country of origin.

visa A permit issued by a country to people it allows in as visitors, or to its own citizens allowing them to leave.

INDEX

Afghanistan 32, 39, 40
Albania 43, 44
Amin, Idi 13-14, 46
asylum 8, 47
Austria 33-34

Berlin 12, 13, 33, 34, 46
boat people 16-19, 22, 31, 46
Britain 7, 12, 14, 32, 34, 43, 44

camps 18-19, 25-29, 33-34, 36
Cherokees 9, 11, 46
China 5, 37, 39, 46
culture shock 21

Dunant, Henri 22

economic refugees 17, 47
El Salvador 5, 28, 43
environmental refugees 14-15
Ethiopia 14, 15, 20, 21, 29, 35, 38, 39

Falashas 20-21, 46
flight from Egypt 10
forced repatriation 18-19, 47
France 6, 7, 10, 12, 32

Guatemala 5, 43
guest-workers 23, 47

Hong Kong 5, 16, 18, 19
host country 17, 47
Huguenots 6, 7, 32, 33, 46

India 37, 39, 40
Indonesia 31
Iraq 24, 40
Israel 10, 20, 21, 26, 27, 34, 46

Khan, Genghis 5, 46
Kurds 24, 26, 41, 45
Kuwait 40

League of Nations 7

Mexico 42, 43
Muslims 6, 40

Nansen, Dr. Fridtjof 8, 46
Nicaragua 43
north-south gap 38

Operation Solomon 20-21, 46

Pakistan 32, 39
Palestine 5, 10, 26, 27, 32, 46

Red Cross 22, 23
Rousseau, Jean-Jacques 10
Russia 5, 8, 12, 38, 39, 43

Spain 6, 12, 23
Swaziland 36

Tamils 43
Thailand 17, 18, 46
Tibet 37, 39

Uganda 13-14, 46
United Nations 8, 14, 17, 20, 23, 25, 26, 27, 36, 42,
   45, 46
United States 7, 11, 12, 14, 18, 19, 23, 30, 32, 33,
   34, 40, 42, 43, 46

Vietnam 5, 16, 17, 18, 19, 22, 31, 32, 46

wars:
   American War of Independence 7, 46
   Arab-Israeli War 26
   First World War 7, 33, 46
   Gulf War 24, 26, 40, 41
   Second World War 4, 8, 12, 23, 33, 42, 46
   Spanish Civil War 12
   Vietnam War 17, 46

Yugoslavia 43